Called to be a Queen not a Fling!

Let's Go, Inc. Dallas, Texas

Library of Congress Cataloguing-in-Publication Data
Bell, Lestine N. (Lestine Nanette), (1974)
You Are Called to be a Queen & Not a Fling! / Lestine N. Bell

ISBN-10 :1514279266

Let's Go, Inc.
www.lestinebellonline.com

Table of Contents

Endorsements

Yakinea Marie Duff
Founder/CEO
Kingdom Entrepreneurs International

"Minister Lestine Bell is an amazing and anointed woman of purpose who is a tremendous blessing to all who encounter her. She is a vessel of hope with the experience, passion, and wisdom to empower the enslaved, broken, and hurting to a place of freedom and wholeness."

Dedication

In memory of my beloved brother Jacob Matthew Bell who passed away too soon. I'm dedicating this project to my brother who thought the world of me and wanted the best for me. You are gone, but not forgotten.

In memory of my beloved grandmother Betsy E. Glasgow who impacted my life beyond words. Thank you, Grandma, for believing in me! Thank you for always telling me how smart I am. Thank you for making me believe I can fly and achieve anything in life. Rest in the presence of the Master until we see each other again.

Acknowledgments

I want to thank God the Father for loving me with such unconditional love and drawing me into a loving relationship with His Son Jesus Christ.

I want to thank my parents, Lester Bell and Mabel J. Jones, for taking me to church as a child and pointing me to the Master Jesus Christ.

I want to thank Dr. Michael D. Moore, my pastor, and spiritual father for teaching me to apply the Word in a practical way. Thank you for showing me what a true shepherd is. Thank you for encouraging me and believing in me. It was your encouragement that gave me the courage to step out and start my ministry.

To my sisters, Tabatha Bell and Sonja Bell Atkins, thank you for your unconditional love and constant encouragement. I love you both!

To everyone who has inspired me on my journey – you know who you are!

Thank You!

Introduction

It is my prayer that this book will:

- Open the eyes of women around the world to embrace their God-given worth;

- Open the eyes of women to never be deceived or settle again when it comes to relationships;

- Help women move from Pain to Purpose;

- Provide the courage to end an unhealthy relationship;

- Help women to awaken to the reality that they have been called to impact the world;

- Encourage women to draw closer to God by putting Him first.

Writing this book to inspire women around the world has been very rewarding and fulfilling. One of my greatest desires in life is to help women be the best woman God has created her to be, by empowering, inspiring, and encouraging her to walk in her greatness. In writing this book I had to reopen the wounds of my past experiences. However, I knew that sharing my story would help so many women to recognize and embrace their true worth. This new found joy I have in my heart comes from knowing the significant number of women who will experience freedom.

My story of overcoming heartache, pain, disappointments, abuse, trauma, and unhealthy relationships was my primary motivation for writing this book. My story is one shared among thousands of other women, the story of triumph that will inspire other women to come out as champions as well. As you read on to the chapters ahead, I pray you receive the healing, inspiration, and encouragement to move forward in life by letting go of the past, healing from unhealthy relationships, and embrace your God given worth by never settling in life. So many woman are still bound by the pain of their past and continue to carry the scars of life from relationships that didn't work out and life experiences. It's time for women to rise up and get up by taking their place in this world as the beautiful Queen God created you to be. I hope and pray that every woman reading will experience revival on the inside, by awakening to her true authentic self. When you are living your true authentic self, by loving yourself, you will never settle for a half-hearted relationship.Women are Queens and should never settle!

Ask yourself the questions below,

- Is this relationship "healthy" or "unhealthy?"

- Does this relationship cause me to compromise sexually by violating God's command to remain sexually pure until marriage?

- How does this man treat me when I'm in his presence?

- Is the relationship about sex only?

- Are we taking this relationship to the next level?

Regardless of what others may think, we all know when we're in a stagnant relationship. We know when a relationship is healthy or unhealthy. We know when we're truly loved by someone or just being misled. The good news is that you don't have to settle anymore! After reading this book, women around the world will begin to embrace their worth and never settle for a half-hearted relationship again. Women are gifts and should never be used or abused by anyone. This book will awaken you to the truth that you are a "Queen" and not a "Fling!"

A "fling" is a man's play thing – someone he has no intentions of making his wife. Ladies, you deserve a ring, you were created to be a man's "Queen," his wife – not just someone he can just have his way with whenever he wants. If you're ready and serious about positioning yourself for a real committed relationship – and not a half-hearted one – then read on. If you're ready to embrace your worth, READ ON! After reading this book, your life will never be the same. You will begin to see yourself as the precious jewel you are. Today is your day! I encourage each of you to move forward from the pain of your past and embrace the bright future that awaits you! It's time for you to be all God has created you to be. You were called to be a Queen, not a Fling!

Chapter 1

"The Pain & Scars of Life"

"The Pain & Scars of Life"

Everyone has experienced the title of this chapter at some point in their lives. Most of us share childhood pain that is still deeply rooted within our hearts and souls as adults. The only difference is that we have learned to mask our pain subconsciously, covering our scars with imaginary bandages that never healed.

As a child, I remember whenever I fell and hurt myself my open wound was covered by a bandage. Then my mother or grandmother would tell me that in order for the wound to heal properly, I had to remove the bandage. This teaching is synonymous with the wounds in our hearts and souls. If we simply cover the pain of our past with an imaginary bandage and never remove it and deal with it, we will never properly heal from the things that scarred us.

For some, you cover your wounds with expensive clothes; expensive cars; a successful career; a dream home; or relationships with men. Regardless of how hard we work to make ourselves seem "successful" on the outside, none of these external things can heal your deeply rooted pain. No amount of money, number of college degrees, or having a man on your arm (who you're sleeping with to numb your pain) can heal you where you hurt. Only the power of God can seep down into the crevices of your heart and heal you from within.

It's God's will that you heal from everything that hurts you. God not only want to heal your heart and restore your soul, He want you to be made completely whole!

So, how did I get here? As a forty year-old woman (and whatever age you are right now), how did we get to the place of extreme pain and being so scarred in our lives? Well, for me it began in childhood. I was violated sexually by a family member - not just once, but many times by the same person. There was another family member who touched me inappropriately by fondling me.

I remember feeling so ashamed and guilty that I carried those secrets with me without telling a soul. As sad as it may sound, whenever a child is violated sexually they often feel as though it is his/her fault. This may not be the case for everyone violated sexually as a child, but drawing upon my story and the stories of other women, it is certainly the case for most.

As mentioned earlier in this chapter, we all know what pain feels like regardless of what caused the pain. We continue carrying scars from our past when we don't deal with what caused our scars. For some, it may be sexual, verbal, and/or physical abuse, abandonment, or rejection – whatever caused the affliction, we must heal. This is necessary for you to live fruitfully and productively, building healthy relationships in the process. I'm sure most of you are saying, "I am already living a productive and fruitful life. I have a successful career; I have money in the bank; I own my own home, etc." But, ladies, we must learn that nothing external heals us of our pain. Only God can heal us at the core of our existence.

Ladies, just because you choose to ignore the pain doesn't mean it will just go away on its own. Issues from our childhood and our lives in general have to be acknowledged and dealt with in order for us to move on to the next phase of our lives successfully.

I'm sure you're asking yourself right now, "Why is she talking about issues from childhood and pain from the past? This book is supposed to be about a woman's worth and relationships!" Well, I'm glad you asked! The pain and hurt of our past affects us in the present. If we allow it and continue to ignore it, it will also negatively affect our future. I've counseled many women who are making bad decisions in relationships because they have yet to deal with the pain of their past. I know for sure when a woman is whole – knowing who she is and her <u>value</u> – she will never allow herself to settle for a relationship that's not conducive to her self-advancement. When a woman is whole, she will <u>not</u> subject herself to a position of a doormat – allowing herself to be taken advantage of and mistreated. She will <u>not</u> allow him to string her along because he's not serious about her. She will <u>not</u> allow him to abuse her on <u>any</u> level. She will <u>not</u> make allowances for mediocre men for the sake of having a relationship. A <u>whole</u> woman knows her worth. She requires respect, honor, and pursuit. If a man, ladies, isn't pursuing you, then he doesn't want you. Period. If you're doing the pursuing, then you don't know your worth.

Consider Proverbs 18:22:

"Whosoever findeth a wife, findeth a good thing, and obtaineth favour of the LORD."

Ladies, if a man truly desire to be with you he will pursue you. God has made it plain in the scripture that a man is to find <u>you</u>. When you are doing the pursuing, you're operating outside of the will of God. When a man know your worth, he will pursue you. Desperate women search for men and are on the prowl for them. Conversely, a woman of virtue requires pursuit because she know her worth.

Think about it. When a woman makes finding a man her top priority, she loses her purpose and her focus is distorted. When we're single, our time is better served discovering our life's purpose.

We must be able to move forward in our purpose and destiny; to become all that God has created us to be; and we must deal with our past issues in order to move forward.

Before moving on to the next chapters, I want to lay the foundation by helping women understand why we attract men who are *abusers* and *users*. Men who use and abuse women are hurting themselves. There's a saying that goes, "Hurt people hurt other people." When you're whole, you won't allow a man to use or abuse you in any way. Women who are walking around with hidden pain and trauma from their past attract men who, too, are walking around with pain in their hearts from their past. Believe it or not, ladies, men can sense vulnerability. If a man senses that you are weak, hurt, timid, or on the rebound, he will say what he thinks you want to hear to get what he wants from you. Your blinders are on, so your emotions prevent you from seeing what you need to see. I pray this message pull all of your broken pieces together, seal them together with the seal of God's powerful healing, so you can move beyond all of the hurtful pain of your past, and never settle in life or relationships.

One thing I want to shout from the rooftop to all women is that you will attract what is hidden in you. Pain attracts pain! It's important that women can step back and take some time to heal. We can no longer continue to pile pain on top of pain. It's time to heal, so you can move forward into your God-given destiny! Carrying around pain from your past can paralyze you, preventing you from becoming all that God has created you to be. I learned this the hard way! My relationships were deeply challenged because of my painful past. When challenges arose in my relationships, instead of dealing with them head on, I preferred to run away from them. I didn't want to experience more pain; I just wanted the feeling of being free. This is also *fear*. I didn't know this was fear, the fear of being hurt caused me to run.

I chose to write about these issues in the first chapter because in order for a woman to fully embrace her worth, she must heal from the pain of her past. Once this is done, she will be able to see herself the way God sees her declaring herself UNSTOPPABLE! Ladies, you are fierce, talented, gifted and beautiful and it's time to deal with your deeply rooted issues, so you can move forward.

- What pain are you still carrying around from your childhood that you've swept under the carpet?

- Were you violated sexually and never said anything to anyone because you thought no one would believe you?

- Were you physically, mentally, or verbally abused as a child?

- What was said to you as a child that you're still struggling to overcome (even now in adulthood)?

- Were you rejected or abandoned as a child?

I'm asking these questions because although so many women have matured into adulthood, they still live with the shame of these issues, causing them to make poor choices in relationships. A woman's behavior in relationships and what she tolerate is often rooted in the lack of a relationship with her Father.

A number of relationship issues are rooted in women relationship with their father, for example. Either her father was absent from her young life, or was present, yet emotionally absent. As a result of his behavior, women are drawn into relationships seeking from a mate what they did not receive from their fathers. This leads to more pain and disappointment. It also lead us to accept mediocrity from our men because we so desperately desire a male's attention and affection – two important things we did not receive from our fathers. Men notice this and proceed with milking us for all they can get! What is the problem with that, you ask? The problem is that men end up with the whole cow without ever paying one dime, thus perpetuating the cycle of hurt and disappointment. We have been looking to a man to give us only what God can give us, and that's complete healing and wholeness! Colossians 2:10 tells us, *"And ye are complete in him, which is the head of all principality and power."* Sex cannot heal your wounded soul regardless of how many men you date. It's only a temporary fix, whereas the restoration that God gives is permanent.

I desire for women to return to their first love – their Creator, God. By returning to your first love, God will love you unconditionally. He will shower you with His love. He will reveal to you His love, showing you what true love is, so when a suitor approaches you, you will love yourself enough to accept only what you deserve as a "Queen" and not a "Fling."

In life I've come to realize that everything has a root cause.The choices and decisions we make in life is a direct reflection of what's going on inside of us. I know that I've personally made some bad decisions in my life that stemmed from a poor self image I had of myself, and not being completely healed from the issues of my childhood. This was my primary reason for addressing the issue of dealing with unresolved pain from the past, because so many women are involved in unhealthy relationships. A wrong relationship can change the course of your life, that can take years to recover from. In order for you to attract a man with substance, character, and Integrity, that will love you, you must heal on the inside first. It was extremely important for me to address this issue to help women understand why they choose and remain in unhealthy relationships. If you're still carrying pain from your childhood or previous relationships that didn't work out, then that's what you'll attract into your life. You will continually attract men that's hurting themselves, and because of their unresolved issues they'll most likely hurt you. The information I'm sharing about men in this book, is not designed to belittle, put down, or demean them in any way. This message of empowerment is to help heal and restore relationships. My mission in writing about the issue of relationships, is to enlighten women about the reality of why men exemplify poor behavior, and what we as women should do to protect ourselves. I don't believe that men are dogs, and it shouldn't be used to address a man under any circumstances. Men are human beings just like we are, but have issues within themselves that need to be addressed and healed as well. Issues from their childhood, lack of self discipline, and poor character. A man that know who he is, his purpose in life, and fear God doesn't have time to play women. Relationships are designed to enhance our lives for good. So keep that in mind with the next man you meet.

Chapter 2

"Counterfeit Love"

"Counterfeit Love"

We all at some point in our lives, dealt with counterfeit love. A counterfeit is *false appearing real*. Normally, we associate the word *counterfeit* with money. Counterfeit money is fake money that appears real and is able to deceive most of its handlers. To the trained eye, however, counterfeit money can be spotted and removed from the rest of the authentic currency. Those who are caught producing and/or using counterfeit money reap varying kinds of consequences, i.e., federal legal action, prison time, loss of employment, and public embarrassment. In relationships, we encounter counterfeits all the time. Counterfeit lovers appear to be real, tricking you into believing that their affection is genuine. Counterfeit lovers tell you what you want to hear in order to get what they want. This information is never disclosed to you – and you end up learning the truth the hard way.

Counterfeit love brings you constant heartache, pain, and disappointment, but you choose to remain in it to avoid being alone. The truth of the matter is that you're doing yourself a great disservice because you're blocking real love from manifesting in your life! In this chapter, you will learn to recognize counterfeit love, and have the courage to let go, to position yourself for real love.

You must understand that you will never receive the true love you deserve from a counterfeit relationship because everything about the relationship is false. It may feel real, but until you learn the tools that will help you distinguish the real from the fake, you will continue in a relationship that does not benefit you. If the foundation of love is truth, then a counterfeit love must be based upon a lie. Ladies, it is impossible to receive true love from the counterfeit!

Indulging in a counterfeit relationship will cost you. Not only will it block you from a real love, it will also cause you to lose time, energy, and focus. The time you're wasting with the counterfeit is valuable and you will never get that time back. This type of relationship will zap your energy with constant pain, heartache, and disappointment. It will exhaust you with the back and forth emotional disappointment and let down. It will also make you lose focus on who you *are*, who you *hope to be*, and whatever dreams you have set for yourself.

It is mind boggling how a woman will waste years of her life with a man she knows doesn't love her to avoid being alone. The real underlying and unspoken reason is that she doesn't know her worth or love herself. For some reason, she may believe that she doesn't deserve a man to love, honor and respect her. She may believe that a genuine man doesn't exist, so she settles for "the man she can get." Every real woman deserves a real man! Think about this: If you knew your worth before wasting your valuable years with a counterfeit, *you would be married by now*! Yes, the truth hurts, but I am here to help you, not chastise you. It's difficult to hear someone tell us about what we are doing wrong in our lives, but instead of rejecting it, I hope you see that I speak to you from a heart of love. I also hope you embrace my message and realize the "Queen" you are. I discussed a few of the reasons why women accept counterfeit relationships , but consider this reason as well. *Many women have never seen an example of true love or experienced it themselves.* What does it look like? What does it feel like? Most of us just don't know! This is why it's so easy to settle for the counterfeit. We must establish a love relationship with God. It is through this relationship that you will begin to understand what true love is, what it looks like, and what it feels like. When you're tempted to settle for a counterfeit relationship, you'll have the wisdom to identify it at the beginning and know your self-worth enough to say, "No I will not settle!

Let's take a look at some attributes of the counterfeit love so you'll be able to discern a counterfeit or know if you're currently dating a counterfeit.

- *Distrusting – envious, possessive, suspicious, accusing, anxious*

- *Betrayal – fickle, inconsistent, double minded, unreliable, unpredictable, wavering, unfaithful, unstable, abusive*

- *Impatient – intolerant, short-tempered, quick to find fault, belittle, or insult with a sharp tongue*

- *Unforgiving – judgmental, disapproving, blaming, condemning, bitter, resentful, hateful, vengeful, vindictive*

These are to name a few of the attributes of counterfeit love. If you are consistently dealing with these attributes, chances are you're with the wrong person.

Let's look at a few attributes of true love.

- *True love is trusting, committed, consistent in loving, not fickle, wavering, or undependable.*

- *True love is kind, gentle, full of grace. It always seeks harmony. It's not harsh, irritable, or mean spirited.*

- *True love is forgiving and merciful. It doesn't look for faults. It doesn't harbor bitterness.*

- *True love is meek and humble.*

- *True love is peaceable. It is not confrontational or contentious. It is not easily offended.*

- *True love serves. Serving is doing something without seeking anything in return.*

Are you ready to receive true love into your life? Are you ready to experience the love you were meant to have, and the love you deserve to have? Then you need to make a decision today to let go of the counterfeit in your life. You need to allow God to cleanse and heal your heart, so you will have room for the real love God has set aside for you. I want each of you to position yourself to receive your King!

In our quest to find love, many women do not guard their hearts as the Bible has instructed us in Proverbs 4:23. The verse gives wise counsel on how to protect yourself, *"Guard your heart with all diligence; for out of it flows the issues of life."*

Guarding your heart does not mean closing yourself off from people and not sharing the love of God. It simply means to use discernment. Through a consistent prayer life and careful study of God's word, you will be sufficiently equipped to recognize a counterfeit.

I want to conclude this chapter with the final details of a counterfeit relationship.

The Counterfeit Man

- *Enjoys ungodly activities.*

- *Draws you away from your relationship with God and steers your focus to him (the counterfeit).*

- *Is very selfish.*

- *Is insensitive towards you and your emotions.*

- *Does not believe the Bible is God's inspired Word*

- *Does not live by the inspired Word of God.*

The God-sent Man

- *Is very passionate about God and God's Word.*

- *Will encourage your relationship with God.*

- *Will make sure you're drawing close to God and not away from Him.*

- *Will give without expecting anything in return from you.*

- *He loves you unconditionally with no hidden motives.*

This was designed to give you ladies a reference on how to detect counterfeit love. I know it will be difficult to cut ties if you're currently tied to a counterfeit, but it's necessary for the sake of your freedom and destiny! Open your eyes and see the trap of being tied to counterfeit love, so God can bring true love into your life. You deserve it!

Chapter 3

"The Other Woman"

Women that settle for being the other woman subject themselves to men that are not only married, but men that are single. but dating someone else. If a man is married, separated, engaged, or dating someone, then he's off limits. If decide to entertain a man that's not available, then you're the other woman or his woman on the side. Knowing your worth ladies will cause you to never settle for this type of relationship. You deserve more in a relationship than being a man's part time lover, You will ultimately get hurt by a man that's not available. You deserve so much more in a ____ relationship. Women that reduce themselves to being the other woman hasn't discovered her true purpose in life. Women that settle for being a man's play thing or secondary in his life, battle with issues from deep within. Every person deserves love in life, but not at the expense of someone else's pain.

First, I want every woman reading this chapter to be honest with yourself. Are you in a relationship with someone who is legally, spiritually, and/or romantically bound to someone else? Are you "the other woman?" Are you in a relationship where you can't be "the" woman – only the "other" woman? If you are in this type of relationship, by the end of this chapter I want you to value yourself enough to break free from this type of bondage.

It was imperative for me to write this chapter because many women around the world hold the title of "the other woman." If a man is seeing you and other women simultaneously, then you are not his "only." Many of women settle and tolerate this kind of behavior because they have unresolved emotional issues that prevent them from valuing themselves. Many of our hearts still need healing! Settling is also indicative of how we view ourselves. We may not deem ourselves worthy of having a man all to ourselves. We may simply accept this behavior because we believe subconsciously that this is a normal male behavior. We may have even witnessed other women in our lives accept similar behavior from men, so we feel reassured that this behavior is acceptable.

It's not your purpose in life to be the other woman and never will be!

What I want women all around the world to understand is that God set aside a man for each woman and vice versa. I Corinthians 7:2 clearly states, *"Nevertheless, because of sexual immorality, let each man have his own wife and let each woman have her own husband."* Here, the Word of God gives a great example and gives specific instructions about every woman having her own husband and not someone else's. When a woman understands her worth, she will know that she deserves her <u>own</u> husband. A woman who has healthy self-esteem will <u>not</u> allow herself to be secondary, and she will definitely not accept this type of disrespect. Seeing, dating, or having sex with a married man is disrespectful and out of order. It's highly disrespectful and deceitful!

We must also consider two additional scriptures. Exodus 20:18, 21 states, *"Thou shalt not commit adultery"* and *"Thou shalt not covet thy neighbor's wife...or anything that is in thy neighbor's house."* When we indulge in the lust of the flesh, whether it is sexual or emotional, we are in direct violation of these two commandments! Not only are we disobeying God's command, we are also enticing another to do the same. This is not what God wants of those He loves.

And, ladies, God loves you!

Men who are separated from their wives are also off limits! Why? They are off limits because God may want to restore the marriage, but when you step in, you are hindering that process by clouding his mind with you and your emotional needs – and not the needs of his estranged wife. They may be separated, but they are still married. Let him get his life in order. God will not violate His Word and send you a man who belongs to someone else. Period!

It's my desire that women all around the world be everything that God has created them to be, maximize their full potential, and be set free. We must also desire that for ourselves.

Remember: We ARE our sisters' keepers!

Genesis 4:9 teaches us that shortly after Cain slew his brother Abel, God asked Cain where Abel was. Cain's sarcastic response was, *"Am I my brother's keeper?"*

In the context of this chapter, we as women can no longer exemplify this type of behavior. Yes, we should be concerned with uplifting our fellow women instead of causing unnecessary and unwarranted heartache and pain by dismantling their family structure. When one woman succeeds at life, we all serve as beneficiaries! Ladies, we must rediscover the unity in womanhood and act accordingly. We should always have our sisters' best interests at heart, serving as their keepers and protectors.
I want you to be so empowered that you will not continue to be so desperate for love and affection that we exact pain on others!

This is a message of awareness - not condemnation.

From the bottom of my heart, ladies, I seek to bring awareness, not condemnation, to this type of behavior. I want us all to find healing and restoration. The Word says in Romans 8:1 that there is no condemnation to those who are in Christ Jesus. Believe me, God desires for us to have the very best and be the very best in our lives! Each of you are called to be a "Queen" and not a "Fling!" Ladies, you deserve a RING, but as long as you settle for being a man's fling
YOU.WILL.NOT.GET.THE.RING!

Don't Get It Twisted!

The Word tells us in Galatians 6:7, *"Do not be deceived, God is not mocked; for whatever a man sows, that he will also reap."* We are quick to gloss over this scripture, but we do need to be reminded of its relevance to our lives. Ladies, imagine this:

> One beautiful sunny Spring day you meet the man of your dreams. He's tall, dark, and handsome as most of us wish. He's educated, well-established, and meets all (or at least most) of your requirements of your ideal mate. After falling madly in love with one another, you marry and begin a family. You begin to praise God for blessing you to be "The Joneses" and not on the sidelines trying desperately to be like "The Joneses." Then, one day out of the blue, you are faced with another woman laying claim to your husband. You also find that she has not only laid

claim, but your husband has given her validity by indulging her desires. The rumor of the affair has been confirmed through tangible proof and the walls of your glass house have come tumbling down.

How would you feel? What would be some of the thoughts running through your head?

Being "the other woman" is a very selfish thing. We are so consumed with our own feelings and desires that we ignore and never consider the wife's feelings. We simply justify our own. As the aforementioned scripture alluded, we have to be careful about what we do. That same thing that we are justifying now will definitely have consequences later!

Remember, this chapter is not to condemn you, but to help heal you from your hurts, so you can realize the "Queen" you are.

What About The Children?

When you cheat with a married man, you are not only breaking the foundation of his marriage, but you are also breaking the innocence of childhood of his children. You should always consider the effects an affair, a divorce, and/or unstable home would have on the children. Statistics have shown that when parents divorce, children endure deep psychological effects that send a ripple effect through the rest of their lives. This may even be an experience you had in your own childhood!

Think about the constant arguing, screaming, swearing that a child might overhear in the aftermath of the affair being brought to light. Consider the strain of a one-parent income that the children may have to undergo because "dad has to sleep at his new apartment." What about the lack of money coming into the household because he is financially supporting and wooing you? Have you thought of how other people's discussion of the affair would affect the child as he overheard people whispering about the affair in church, school, grocery store, etc.? Have you even considered how this one affair would cause the child to be so emotionally discombobulated that their grades begin to suffer and even become physically abusive to others (i.e., school fights) or to themselves (i.e., drugs)?

Cheating does not only affect you, but many other people who are in the picture – including the husband.

Number Seven: The Man, Too

Before I begin this section, let me tell you that I do believe the man shares responsibility for this affair, too! By no means am I giving men a pass here. If a man is entices and encourages you to be with him knowing his own personal status, then he is just as at fault as we are for interrupting his marriage/relationship.

Ladies, here are a few questions we must address:

- If he truly loves me the way that he says he does, why am I "the other woman?"

- How is he respecting me as a woman, or as a woman he supposedly loves, by having multiple women?"

- We must think to ourselves, ladies, how can he love

me with his whole heart if his heart is divided amongst two or more women?

- How am I valued in this?

- Why would he string me on convincing me that he will leave his wife for me when he knows he has no intentions of leaving?"

The million dollar question is,

"Why would you believe him?"

Now That You Are Armed With The Truth, What Should You Do?

You have to sever all ties with him. Yes, it will be difficult to end emotional, habitual, and financial ties to him, but in order for healing and restoration to take place, this severance must happen. Delete his number, change your phone number, Ignore his many advances to 'get you back.' Rid yourself of anything that reminds you of him. It's never easy to break an emotional bond with someone, but because this type of relationship is out of order with what God desires for your life, you must end this relationship completely!

It is natural for us to desire love and to be loved. It's very understandable. However, God does not intend for us to interrupt what He has for two other people – just to have the feeling ourselves. The love we are looking for has to come from God first. It may sound cliché, but God gave us the perfect example of love when He sent His Son to be our

Savior. Not only that, the first relationship we learn of in the Bible, Adam and Eve's, went perfectly fine until a third party became involved!

And, by no means, am I telling you to give him an ultimatum of leaving his wife for you. This is not severing the relationship! Men very seldom ever leave their wives for the women with whom they engage in an affair. Yes, you will hear him say that he will leave his wife for you over and over again (and it will sound like music to your ears), but women all over the world can attest that the record never changes! Consider this, if the man cheated on his wife to be with you, how can you trust that he won't do the same to you?

The time you are wasting fawning over this married man could be more wisely spent with a man who is single and emotionally available. You could be in the process of building a relationship with your own future husband that could possibly lead to your "happily ever after." Don't block your blessings while lying in a mess!

Summing It Up:

Ladies, when you embrace the love of God and allow Him to love and heal you, you'll be ready to receive love from a man the right way. The first step to being free is to repent, sincerely asking the Lord to forgive you. I John 1:9 says, "He's faithful and just to forgive our sins and cleanse us from all unrighteousness." Once you've repented from your wrongdoings, the severance of the relationship we discussed above must occur. You must embrace your worth and value, never settling again for a half-hearted relationship.

I wrote this chapter so you can position yourself to meet a

great man who will love you and treat you like the "Queen" you are. I don't think it's by chance that you're reading this book. God wants to set you free from all these worldly shenanigans and move you into your destiny and purpose. I believe this book was divinely put in your hand so you can wake up and embrace your God-given worth and receive the love you deserve. God is using this book as a revival among women around the world to restore and heal the hearts of his daughters.

Ladies, when you embrace the love of God and allow Him to love and heal you, you'll be ready to receive love from a man the right way. The point I desire to articulate on this topic of being the other woman, is that no matter how you try and rationalize it in you mind, if you're the other woman in a man's life, that simple means your not the apple of his eyes, or his Queen! If your were the center of his world you will not be secondary in his life. When a man is serious about you, you will be a priority and not an option. Period!

Chapter 4

"Flinging"

"Flinging"

Ladies you must wake up to the reality that once you lose the respect of a man, it is extremely difficult to regain it.

If it's easy to get – it's not valued!

Consider this: If diamonds were easily accessible to all people, then they would lose their value to us. We'd simply move to the next inaccessible jewel. We are diamonds, ladies, and Jesus has paid a high price for us. We cannot continue to give discounts on our priceless jewels! This is why it's very important that you set your standards and boundaries in the beginning of every relationship and maintain them. Setting boundaries simply mean you're conveying what you will or will not tolerate, specifically having *casual sex without a commitment* . This boundary should be established at the onset of the relationship, because once you open the door to sex, it is definitely hard to close!

Now, let's define "fling." A fling is man's play thing – someone he passes through until he finds his Queen. He is not serious about the "fling." She's just his "in the meantime girl." He doesn't love her and not serious about her. A "fling" is a woman a man love having sex with, which is the main reason he keep her around. He may enjoy her company, but only when it's convenient for him.

I know some of you are reading this chapter and thinking, "I am not a 'Fling!' This chapter can't be about me because I am a 'Queen!'" There's no reason to be embarrassed and admit to yourself that you probably once a man's "fling." Many women around the entire world have been in this situation multiple times, but we have to find the strength to rid ourselves of relationships that fail to honor our first-class status. This is an issue that has plagued our gender for a long time, and the first step of our recovery from "flinging" is to admit that we are in this type of relationship.

Here are a few questions to ask yourself when trying to determine if you are a man's "fling." Do you have a man who

- Only calls you late at night, but never in the daytime?

- Only texts you, but never talk to you directly?

- Squirms his way out of spending public time with you?

- Dodges relationship and commitment questions with "I'm not ready" or "I like things the way they are" or even the infamous "My last relationship was terrible, so I'm not ready for a new relationship?"

- Refuses to introduce you to his world: his friends, family, co-workers?

- Does not introduce you as his woman in the event that you two encounter someone he know personally?

Think about it: When a man is serious about you and see a future with you, HE WILL LET THE WORLD KNOW!

Deep in your heart , you must admit that you want more than this substandard treatment. I am standing in agreement with you because I know that you <u>are</u> worth more! When you allow yourself to be a man's "fling," you're <u>settling</u>. God didn't create a special person who meets all of your needs for you to waste your time on someone who refuses to give you the love you deserve!

The "Y" Path

The "Y" Path in a relationship, or in this case a situation of "flinging" ("flinging" is not a real relationship because you are not the wife or the primary woman), is when two people start on the same path, but end up going in two separate directions. The woman may desire a real relationship, but because the man is uninterested in solidifying their union with commitment, they end up traveling separate paths. The woman then settles for the sex only relationship and stay in it, they go in two different emotional directions, forming a "Y."

This "Y" Path is confusing! If you think it's confusing here, imagine living it in reality. Confusion is caused by mixing darkness with light – two things that should not co-exist. Confusion comes when the two are forced to stay in the same space. We know that light and darkness cannot coexist scientifically, so why should we try to make light and darkness co-exist in our relationships?

The Word tells us in I Corinthians 14:33 that *"God is not the author of confusion, but of peace."* God want us to have peace in our lives. He doesn't want us to be so consumed with nonsense that we cannot focus our attention on Him. However, we find ourselves in this situation more times than we would like to admit. If peace does not reside in your relationship, then this is an indicator that you're tied to the wrong person! You are not the wife. You are not the girlfriend. You are not his one and only. YOU ARE A FLING!

We Know the Truth, But Choose to Believe A Lie

What's even more tragic is that most women know when a man is not serious about them, but will accept the little attention he gives, in hopes that more will come in the future. However, what happens is that you are subconsciously teaching him that you will accept his shoddy behavior and that he does not have to do more. And, believe me, when you accept his shenanigans, he will <u>not</u> do more. We have to stop falling in love with men for the potential <u>we</u> think they have and instead grow to love the men they are – <u>provided</u> that they're single and available.

You will find yourself in a very precarious position every time because he will tell you what you want to hear just to string you along when he honestly does not desire to commit too you. We've seen a plethora of warning signs throughout the entire experience with this man, but we desire to have the fairytale we've dreamed of since childhood, to the point we can't see that we're living a nightmare. This is a familiar situation to women all around the world, including me, but we have never seen those words written on paper. We have never been taught about the game men play, so we end up on the losing end of the field. I am writing this book because I've been there, and to equip you with the necessary tools to overcome counterfeit relationships, that only consider you as their "fling."

Are you still wondering if you are a "fling?" Check out the following list. A "fling" is:

- A man's plaything; she's his "in the meantime" girl.

- Someone a man is not serious about (and doesn't have plans to be serious about in the future).

- Someone a man love having sex with, but will not commit to or marry.

- Someone who will not get the ring.

- Someone who will not be introduced to his world.

- Someone who is easily manipulated when having sex outside of the will of God.

You will never become the "Queen" when you're a "Fling." In the back of the man's mind, he will always make the connection of the "behind the scenes" woman with you and will never see you in the light that you deserve. The standards you set in the beginning of your relationship will stand for the duration of the relationship. So, ladies, when you set your standards, don't be afraid to set them high! Also, don't be persuaded to lighten up on your standards because counterfeit lovers will always persuade you to bend your standards to accommodate their mediocrity.

Key Note: When you bend, prepare to be broken!

Most importantly, we must remember that men tend to revere those things that are seemingly unattainable; things that are "hard to get;" and things that other men don't have. If you give in easily and freely, he'll quickly move on to the next – or keep you around until his Queen arrives.

The last point I would like to convey in this chapter, is about the importance of establishing a solid friendship before anything romantic. Knowing the difference between friendship vs. flingship (I made that word up myself)! You can't be a man's friend and his fling at the same time, you can't be both. I personally think male and females alike has missed in this area, n building a healthy friendship first before anything else. Friendship is the key in building a healthy relationship, it's the foundation, the glue that will sustain the relationship whenever they encounter challenges or rough spots. Friendship should be the focus when you first meet someone. I often see women skipping this step of establishing friendship first, began having sex, and left with a broken heart. The difference of being a man's fling verses his friend is someone he admire, respect, someone he can talk to by sharing his dreams and goals with. A friend is someone he trust, feel safe, and vulnerable with if he's experiencing challenges in his life. He can trust you with the good and the bad. When you're establishing friendship there should be no sex involved. Sex clouds your mind when you need to make a decision concerning a man's character. On the other hand if you're a man's fling he only enjoy having sex with you without committing to you. Some people call it a friend with benefits. Ladies, you can't give too much of yourself and expect a man to commit to you, because he mostly likely will take his time. Set your boundaries and stick with them!

Chapter 5

"How to Break Unhealthy Sexual Soul-Ties"

"How to Break Unhealthy Sexual Soul-Ties"

Why Sex Before Marriage Is Damaging

Ladies, when you engage sexually with a man who's not your husband, your self-esteem, confidence, and dignity will hit the floor just as fast as your clothes! You will lose who you really are because you will be working overtime trying to please him in hopes that you will get his heart in return. Wake up, ladies! You cannot set your hopes on getting a man's whole heart after you have introduced (and even 'reintroduced') yourself to him in the bedroom. He will not respect you as a woman with whom he could fall in love. When you win men over sexually, he is telling you that 1) he does not expect more because that's where you have set the bar, and 2) he is only coming back for more because the sex is good – not because he is falling in love with you.

- Have you ever wondered why men are able to sleep with several women without having any emotion towards either of them?

- Have you ever wondered why a woman ends up hurt and disappointed after she had given herself sexually to a man?

Women are emotional beings, whereas men are physical beings.. Women tend to think and believe that satisfying a man's flesh will cause him to love them, but instead it only brings heartache. Simply put: Women expect to receive true *love*, but only receive true *lust*.

Men, on the other hand, are driven by the physical, however, that drive doesn't always equal *interest beyond the physical*. Most men will admit, albeit amongst their male friends, that they never planned to commit to a relationship with a woman who was his "fling." He may have planned to commit to calling her in the late night hours, but committing to her in the daytime in a legitimate relationship was never in his plan.

If a man is interested in a relationship, what wins him over is his spiritual and mental connection with a woman. Great sex – in terms of marriage - is just icing on the cake! Note: When baking a cake, the icing is not mixed in with the eggs, sugar, and milk. Instead it is added after the cake has been mixed, baked, and cooled. Ladies, don't give up the icing – or offer a taste – before you give him the cake!

In this chapter, we will explore the power of sex in a relationship and learn why it is important to reserve your body for your husband (and definitely not anyone else's).

What is a Soul-Tie and How is It Developed?

First, let's understand what the soul is. The soul is the mind, the will, and the emotion. Every human being has a soul, spirit, and body. Although the soul and spirit of man can't be seen with natural eyes, it is the very essence of who we are. Matthew 26:26 states, *"For what profits a man to gain the whole world and lose his soul?"* More simply put: What will you really gain when you sell your soul to the devil? Whether we know or admit it, our souls are vital assets to us. We must be mindful of the choices we make in life because they will positively or negatively affect our souls.

Key Point: *Having sex outside of marriage has a negative effect on our souls.*

Sin devastates the mind and soul. When we sin, it devastates God! The very thing that separates us from God is sin, and if we aspire to be holy women of God, we have to resist temptation! Ladies, sin also wounds the soul. The only one who can heal us of that wound is none other than Jesus Christ! To become whole again we must commune with God and re-establish our relationship with Him. We must repent of our sins, praying in the fashion of Psalms 41:4, which states: *"Lord, be merciful to me; Heal my Soul for I have sinned against you…"* And I implore you to resist temptation just as the Word speaks of in I Peter 2:11: *"Beloved I beg you as sojourners and pilgrims, abstain from fleshly lusts which war against the soul."* Doing so will release that devastation, purify you, and open you up for the destiny that God has prepared for you.

Now let's get to the meat of the message!

Here are some very powerful statements that will surely deliver and heal you. The foundational passage of scripture for the power statements is from I Thessalonians 4:1-8, which reads

> *Furthermore then we beseech you, brethren, and exhort you by the Lord Jesus, that as ye have received of us how ye ought to walk and to please God, so ye would abound more and more. For ye know what commandments we gave you by the Lord Jesus. For this is the will of God, even your sanctification, that ye should abstain from fornication: That every one of*

you should know how to possess his vessel in sanctification and honour; Not in the lust of concupiscence, even as the Gentiles which know not God: That no man go beyond and defraud his brother in any matter: because that the Lord is the avenger of all such, as we also have forewarned you and testified. For God hath not called us unto uncleanness, but unto holiness. He therefore that despiseth, despiseth not man, but God, who hath also given unto us His Holy Spirit.

Key Point: Sex outside marriage is abuse to your body.

Wherefore God gave them over to the sinful desires of their hearts to sexual impurity for the degrading of their bodies with one another. They exchanged the truth of God for a lie, and worshipped and served created things rather than the Creator who is forever praised. (Romans 1:24-25)

When you engage in sexual relations with another individual outside of marriage, you are abusing your temple (your body). Body abuse is just like substance abuse. When you are addicted to a substance (i.e., alcohol, cigarettes, drugs), it may feel good in the moment, but it has negative repercussions on the body and the mind later. The same happens when you engage sexually with someone you are not married to. It may feel good in the moment, but the repercussions are long lasting!

Key Point: Our bodies are divine.

Our bodies are physical vessels where the Spirit of the Lord is to dwell. We are to house the glory and very essence of Him within us. It becomes troublesome when our bodies are overflowing with filth! If we are to live as believers, we must be careful of "who" and "what" we invite in.

Consider Matthew 21:12-13:

> *Jesus went into the temple, and began to cast out them that sold and bought in the temple, and overthrew the tables of the moneychangers, and the seats of them that sold doves; And would not suffer that any man should carry any vessel through the temple. And He taught, saying unto them, Is it not written, My house shall be called of all nations the house of prayer? But ye have made it a den of thieves.*

When Jesus came into the temple and saw moneychangers dealing inside of the temple of God, He overturned their tables! He did so because their actions defiled God's temple and did not exalt His Father. They were focused on things that were not pertaining to His Father or His will and Jesus refused to put up with that blatant disregard and disrespect of His Father's House.

Key Point: Body abuse is when you engage sexually with multiple partners.

Consider I Corinthians 6:16:

Do you not know that he who unites himself with a prostitute is one with her body? For it is said, the two will become one flesh.

Promiscuity is not in God's plan for His people! Just as doctors tell us that when we sleep with one person, we inevitably "sleep" with everyone that person has slept with (in terms of the spreading of diseases), the same is true for us spiritually. Doctors give us the physical disadvantages of having multiple sex partners, but let me give you the spiritual disadvantages:

When you sleep with a man, you take on the spirits and/or the bondage of that person you're sleeping with. And speaking of promiscuity, imagine the amount of bondage you will inherit when you sleep with multiple people in bondage!

This revelation of truth brings us to the following power statement.

Sexual sin is when you violate the covenant of God's Word, and as a result it brings guilt, condemnation, and wounding of the soul.

Key Point: The soul and the mind are one.

We all know what is right and wrong, even when it comes to the commandments of the Bible. When we sin against God, our soul and mind begins to respond. It responds by reminding you that you have sinned. Feelings of guilt begin to arise and you begin to have a myriad of emotions. Feelings of condemnation comes because you know you intentionally sinned (you knew that your actions were sinful beforehand) and now you nervously await punishment. These feelings begin to wound your soul and make you feel weary.

Ladies, the second book in the Bible commands us not to commit adultery and even not to covet anything in another's house, i.e., someone else's husband. The Bible speaks against fornication, too. The Bible is the divinely written Word of God given to provide instruction to His people. When we accept God into our lives, this becomes a covenant (an agreement) between us and God that we promise to abide by the commands written therein.

No, we are not perfect, by far, but when we give our lives to God, we should aspire to become the best Christians we can possibly be!

Having a sexual soul-tie with a person who God never intended for you to be connected or tied to will delay or abort your destiny.

Key Point: I discussed this in length in the previous chapters, so I won't belabor the point. However, it is a point I want you to keep in mind.

Too many times we are tired of being lonely, so we end up with someone who is not our destined mate. When we have a sexual soul-tie with someone, we become emotionally attached to them. We want their attention and affection. We long for it. We continue on in the sexual relationship hoping and praying that a true relationship will come. In the meantime, we experience children with the counterfeit lover. We experience heartache and pain from him because he refuses to commit. We stress ourselves out with this "relationship" so much so that our demeanor changes.

The person we once were is no longer the person we see in the mirror. Who we see is so unrecognizable that when we are approached by Mr. Right, we are so far left that we can't turn around in time to be ready to present ourselves to him. Detours distract you from your charted life path and can have grave consequences. Ladies, save yourself the heartache by preparing yourself for The Call, The Purpose, and The Assignment that God has for you!

When you have sex outside marriage, your soul is filled with images of the man/woman you're having sex with and not the image of Jesus Christ.

When we allow our minds to roam, it is very likely that they will roam into the wrong territory. Once they have landed in that sinful land, it makes it even more tempting to act upon those sinful thoughts. That's why we must counteract that mental roaming by adjusting our focus back onto Christ Himself.

Romans 12:2 teaches us, *"And be not conformed to this world: but be ye transformed by the renewing of your mind, that ye may prove what is good, and acceptable, and perfect, will of God."*

If we are to be true vessels and believers in God, we have to change our thoughts to holy ones, and our focus to God.

To take it a little further even, consider II Corinthians 10:5:

Casting down arguments and every high thing that exalts itself against the knowledge of God bringing every thought into captivity to the obedience of Christ.

Key Point: When you're having sex outside marriage it's difficult to gaze upon and focus on the Holy One of Israel, the Lord Jesus Christ.

This type of relationship set up idols in your life and heart. Exodus 20:3 explicitly states, *"Thou shalt have no other gods before me."* When we hear this we automatically bypass this because we think that since we are not worshipping a "god" of another religion, this doesn't apply to us. However, a god, or idol, is <u>anything</u> that we place before God. It can be a job, a celebrity, person – and in most of our cases, we will put a man before God. We will tend to the needs of a man here on earth, but won't spend time with God in prayer and study of His Word. God tells us in Exodus 20:5 that He is *"…a jealous God."* He wants our attention,

Ladies, if you give God what He is due, He will bless you beyond measure!

Warning
This is about to get graphic, ladies!

When you lift your arms towards Heaven, you're surrendering yourself completely to the Lord. Likewise when you open your legs to a man, you are surrendering to that man – giving all of you to him. A man.

When you surrender yourself to man that you're not married to sexually and he walks away, you feel devastated because you have given your all to him. You feel that a part of you has been stolen from you that cannot be replaced. Men are *givers* and women are *receivers*. This is why a man can sleep with a woman and have no emotional attachments.

Women are very emotional, even more so that men. This is why women are getting hurt, wounded, rejected, and used because you're opening yourself up and surrendering to the <u>wrong</u> person in the <u>wrong</u> way. The only way your body should be stretched out is in a position of worship and laying prostrate on the floor before the Lord.

When you have sex outside marriage you will be easily manipulated and deceived . The soul-tie between you and your counterfeit lover will latch on and hold for dear life – and will refuse to let go!

You know God is not pleased with this relationship or behavior, but you don't let go because you're too far in. When we engage in sex, especially sinful sex (not with our <u>own</u> husbands), it will seem as though it is the best you ever had. This is a trick of the enemy to keep you entangled in a sin that you should not be caught in in the first place! This trick of the enemy will entice you to return to get that same feeling.

Ladies, don't be tricked by the sex!

**Sex outside marriage feels like love, but it's lust.
Fornication is driven by lust.**

To keep #5's message going, we must be strong enough to decipher between love and lust. Let's begin with love. To understand what true love is, we must know the love of Christ and the love that He so freely gives each of us. This love, although divine and unconditional, can be reciprocated in earthly love between two people. Now, lust is different than love, but is often confused with it. It's a carnal love. It loves from the physical body, most popularly the "reproductive area." Conversely, when people love one another, they love from the heart and soul.

To give you a better understanding of lust, consider this acronym:

Living Under Satan's Torment

When you have violated your body with adultery and fornication, the feelings of guilt and condemnation will consume you. You will be tormented by Satan, which means YOU.WILL.HAVE.NO.PEACE!

Secrecy breeds deception.

Please note that your secret sin is <u>not</u> secret to God! God sees all and He knows all, so please make no mistake about Him knowing your sin! Consider the story of Adam and Eve in the Bible. After Eve and Adam partook of the fruit of the forbidden tree, God let the two know that He knew what they'd done. After Cain's murder of his brother Abel, God soon let Cain know that He knew His secret.

When you secretly sin men are able to deceive you. You are alone with him only and you don't have the backing of a friend whose eyes are open to the reality of the situation. You are blinded by lust masquerading as love. Check out the acronym for secret:

Satan Eliminating Christ Revelatory Eternal Truths

Ladies, I want you to think about this. If you are a secret, the other women he's dealing with doesn't know about you and you don't know about them. And, believe me, he does <u>not</u> want you – or them - to find out about his dirty work under the covers!

And, in none other but Jesus' name, do I bind up this lying and deceiving spirit that's counseling the minds of God's people to keep them in bondage!

Men, when you have sex with a woman outside marriage, you are misleading her.

Men, God has positioned you as the head of the household – not just in a controlling manner – but as the person who is to lead the family in the right direction under direct guidance of the Lord. When you abandon your home and engage with a woman you are not married to, you are out of order and out of the will of God.

You are misleading her in because you are missing the leading of the Lord. If you were following the leading of the Lord, you will not lead her to your bed. You should instead lead her to Christ! If she is not your wife, you should lead her to the path to finding her own husband.

A married man or woman is off limits! Period. Having sex or even dating someone who is married is unscriptural and it devastates families.

I have dealt with this throughout the book so far, but it is a power statement in itself. Don't lead yourself into temptation by engaging in a relationship with a married man. Platonic friendships are fine, but once you see that the platonic relationship is taking a left turn – on your part or his – you need to straighten it back out again for the sake of your soul.

You may believe that if you bend a little and say, go to lunch or dinner alone with him you will be okay. However, doing so is a lead in for feelings to begin to develop and soon you will find yourself in a situation that will be hard to escape.

I want to end this chapter by providing you with a prophetic prayer to break soul–ties.

- *I DECLARE that the people of God rise to their prophetic destiny.*

- *I COMMAND the lust demon to come up and out in the name of Jesus!*

- *I COMMAND every unclean spirit of fornication, masturbation, group sex – every form of sexual perversion to come up and out by the power and the authority of Jesus' name!*

- *I COMMAND your soul to be restored from every sexual encounter that you've ever had with any person that you were not married to.*

- *I COMMAND Satan to release the grip of your soul NOW!*

- *I DEMAND that Satan no longer torment your mind with lustful thoughts in Jesus Name.*

I take authority over sexual soul-ties that have our people bound, I bind it, and loose them now! I break them once and for all, in Your Holy Name Jesus! I loose it from your people and decree that it cannot reform this day or any day to come, I bind Satan and all of his evil ministering spirits that he sends out to his work in Jesus' name. I call your people cleansed of their history and of this defilement in the Holy Name of Jesus!

Amen. Amen. Amen!!!

Chapter 6

"Called to be a Queen"

"Called to be a Queen"

You Are Worth the Wait

God created women to be Queens and desire for us to be respected as such. You are beautiful, powerful, and worthy. We have to believe each of those things about ourselves before we can expect others to treat us accordingly. I want you to write down five positive attributes you aspire to have on a sheet of paper. Every morning when you are freshening up in the mirror, I want you to speak those attributes. For example,

I am strong. I am independent. I am successful. I am confident. I am worth the wait!

Repeat this daily for an extended period of time. Over time, you will begin to attribute each characteristic to yourself. What is the point of repeating this? Read the fifth statement. *I am worth the wait.* Repeating your personalized mantra will convince you that you embody each adjective about yourself. Every negative thing anyone has every spoken to you and over your life will be turned over and will be made void. You are a Queen. You are worth fighting for. And, besides, if you don't believe 5 simple positive things about yourself, how can convince someone else?

Where does the sense of worth come from?

Our worth as human beings comes from God - be it male or female. Psalms 139:14 says, *"I will praise You for I am fearfully and wonderfully made. Marvelous are your works, and that my soul knows very well."*

We are wonderfully made. We are unique beings who were handcrafted by God Himself. This, alone, gives us worth!

Let's dig a little deeper into understanding our worth. We must first understand the power of our Creator. The first book of the Bible, Genesis, teaches us that God is so powerful that He simply spoke light into existence. He created man from the dust of the ground and simply blew life into him. When man couldn't tend to the Garden of Eden alone, God caused a deep sleep to come over him, removed his rib, and created him a helpmate: the woman. Knowing that God is almighty and omnipotent and He created you – that alone should give you a sense of your worth! You are one of His many magnificent creations!

Many times we look for acceptance and approval from men, other women, family, co-workers, etc. But believe me, ladies, NO other human being has the power to give us worth because it is a gift that only God can give!

This revelation absolutely excludes man from ever taking any credit as the governing authority on a woman's worth. For worth to be bestowed, it must come from a higher authority.

We must also consider Genesis 1:21, which tells us, *"God created man in own image; in the image of God He created Him. Male and female He created them."* We were created in His own image, so we must learn to see ourselves through His eyes. Being created in the image of God is the highest honor bestowed upon mankind.

Simply put, worth is having value, excellence of character, and importance. You are very important to God, which is why He created you. And, ladies, whatever has happened in your past that has distorted this revelation, I pray, will be eradicated by the time you finish reading this book.

God used me a vessel to write this book to awaken His precious daughters to their God-given purpose. If you've lost your sense of worth through trials, negative circumstances, bad relationships, and trauma of a painful past, God wants to heal and restore you to wholeness.

- *Are you currently in a relationship that compromises who you are?*

- *Are you in a relationship that diminishes your sense of self worth?*

- *Does the relationship edify you as a person and encourage you to be all that God created you to be?*

- *Does the relationship leads to continual disobedience to God's Word?*

- *Does the relationship cause you to compromise sexually or cause you to compromise your godly values?*

If you are in a relationship where you are consistently compromising, it will cause you to view yourself in a negatively. This is characteristic of both sin and compromise - it clouds and distorts our view of ourselves. If you are compromising in a relationship, then you are in an unhealthy relationship. How are you compromising? You are compromising *sexually*. Engaging in sex before marriage is not in God's plan for us. However, we do so all the time hoping to keep men interested in us, thinking they will want to keep us long term. Ladies, you are worth the wait and you don't have defile your body to keep a man's attention.

As we discussed in Chapter 2, we settle for half-hearted relationships because fear of being alone or being without a man. This is unhealthy! We must overcome the fear of being alone and learn *patience*. We must have faith that God will give us a man who is worthy of our love and who also has a pure motive. Anyone who diminishes your self-worth should not have the honor of sharing your space. We can no longer allow our self-esteem and self-worth to be diminished or damaged by men who don't value us. The man who God has for every woman reading this book will enhance your life in every way. He will use that man to increase you, love you, respect you, and adore you. This man will not tear you down in any way. If there's constant disrespect, lack of commitment and lack of trust, then it's time to re-evaluate the relationship.

And, ladies, if you realize that your current man does not increase you, then don't be afraid to end that relationship. It's not about being mean, or "hating all men," etc., it's about getting what you deserve. If he's not willing to give you what you deserve, then give him what he deserves: THE DOOR.

God revealed to me that a woman's worth is her wealth. When a woman allows someone or something to diminish her worth, she hinders her wealth from flowing into her life. The acronym for worth is (When Our Reality Takes Hold). Whenever a woman fully embraces her worth her wealth will follow. Don't be mistaken. Wealth is not *external*, but *internal*. Every human being has worth. Your worth doesn't come from anything external, i.e., relationships, money, education positions, status - or the lack thereof. A woman's wealth comes from knowing her worth and who she is as a person and as a woman of many gifts and talents. It is those God-given gifts and talents that will bring wealth to that individual.

Ladies, I am saying this to you because I believe that I have a divine call to inspire others to reach their full potential. Women are losing themselves; not loving themselves; are settling; are dealing with unimaginable pain that they cannot escape. Women are existing in survival mode, which prevents women from writing that book God put inside them; starting that business that you wanted to start; ministering to others that God has called you to do; or achieving any of the many goals God has put in their hearts. I come today to let you know that it's not too late. It's not too late to fulfill your dreams. Today is the day that you need to decide that you are worth true love. You are worth getting married to the man of your dreams who feels the same about you. You are worth seeing yourself positively – and not negatively.

It was in the Garden of Eden that a woman's view of herself was distorted by the enemy. When a woman's view of herself is distorted, it's because she has taken her focus off God. This causes her to become self-conscious, insecure, and feel inferior. This Satan Initiated Negativity (SIN) not only causes our self-image to become distorted, but is so strong that we spend extended amounts of time under its control. But don't fret, ladies, because God has the power to overcome all obstacles whether it originates on earth or in hell!

Conclusion

What's a Queen? A Queen is a woman who understands who she is. She is confident; has high self-esteem; and she understands her worth and value. A Queen rules and reigns in life and handles her business. She has influence with strong character and integrity.

Let's look at the attributes of a *virtuous woman* as outlined in the Bible. She was a Queen, indeed! After reading of The Proverbs 31 Woman, you will not be the same and you will walk and live as the Queen that you are.

Proverbs 31:10 reads, *"Who can find a virtuous woman? For her price is far above rubies."* A true Queen, indeed!

A Queen is different from the rest. She:

- Stand out above others.

- Doesn't put herself out to be seen by a man - she must be found.

- Is kind and uses her tongue wisely – only to lift and build her man up.

- Is Godly and loved all who know her.

- Is of a cheerful countenance for her heart and motives are pure.

- Is royalty and dresses accordingly.

- Is rare and not easily discovered.

- Will only recognized by a real King.

- Requires pursuit and refuses to pursue a man.

- Is not attracted to a man for his money or worldly possessions, but instead his character.

Is this you? Yes, it is! This is why you shouldn't settle. You are a Queen, indeed. Now, get ready to be found by your King!

Chapter 7

"Created to be Whole"

"Created to be Whole"

God created you to be whole. The trauma of negative experiences, child abuse, fractured relationships, homes broken through divorce, and negative self portraits of ourselves have had a profound effect on all of us. Being wounded in our early year has affected our decision making in relationships. The aftermath of bad experiences persist throughout our lives. We've hoped that time will heal all of our pain, but this is not the case. If time healed all of our pain, we would all be healed right now. What time does for our pain is simply slide it out of the way a little, but it doesn't actually disappear – but just simply moves out of view. We must confront our pain in order to overcome it and to become whole in the name of Jesus.

Trauma

Trauma from our past robs us of portions of our lives. It robs us our true identity and our peace. When a person has been traumatized as a child (or even as an adult), she tends to carry around unresolved hurt. Trauma isolates us and leaves us feeling as though God has nothing good or positive for us. This is why I'm closing this book with the revelation that "we are created to be whole" because when you're whole, you make better choices in life. When you're whole, you will be drawn to whole people. When you're whole, you will not allow a man to abuse you or use you.

Wholeness Comes from God

The answer to our hurt and pain is God and allowing Him to love you with His unconditional love. Your Heavenly Father wants you to know He loves you. He has the power to heal you of your painful past and all the mistakes you've ever made in your life. God has the power to deliver you from being scarred by tragic experiences, so they won't continue to have lasting effects on you. Let God come in and heal you with His love and compassion for you. Allow God to restore your loss of identity, heal your wounded heart, and redeem your life. You are not what you experienced as a child. So many women have lost hope in love and life because of their terrible past, but today is a new day and the start of a new season!

Isaiah 43:18-19 states,

> Do not remember the former things nor consider the things of old. Behold, I will do a new thing, now it shall spring forth. Shall you not know it? I will even make a new way in the wilderness and rivers in the desert.

Ladies, God is doing a new thing in your life and heart. This is your new season and your new life! I declare that all women reading this book will no longer allow childhood tragedies, histories of broken relationships, and despair for the future hinder you from being whole and moving forward into your purpose. The scar-producing pain of your past will no longer affect your decisions when it comes to relationships. The pain of your past is no longer the blueprint for your present and the vision God has for your future.

Deliverance

It is deliverance from the misery of our past that brings hope and healing. This is what every human being needs and only God can manifest that into our lives. When we're not whole, it hinders our relationships – with God and man – your dreams, and also your ability to fulfill your dreams and goals. Draw near to a loving relationship with God today. This is where you will find rest from your hurts and pain. This is where you will see your renewed vision for your life. God loves you and will never abandon you. He will bind up your wounds and passionately remove your scars – making way for a new, whole, beautiful Queen. He wants you to live your best life now! Get ready to enter into a place of completion, of wholeness.

To elaborate a little more on a point I made at the top of this chapter, we have learned to find coping mechanisms on our own – without the counsel of Christ. We usually push the traumatic situation to the back of our minds and believe that we will get over it through forgetting it. But, ladies, this doesn't work! In order to be delivered from a pain, we have to give it over to Jesus. So many of us have been emotionally paralyzed hurt and disappointment, but Jesus is known to be a miracle worker! If we have faith in His power and His love for us, He is sure to come in and turn our lives around!

God is bringing order out of the chaos that you've been living in. God is restoring what has been stolen from you and desires to place you in a position of dominion and power.

Jesus was sent by God to bring healing and freedom to us. He came to deliver us from our wounds and scars. He came to restore our finances. And, believe me, He is able to do the impossible! He wants you to be free from the chains of your confining mindset. If you will look to Jesus, you will lack nothing because He will supply every one of your needs. That even includes a husband, your own husband, who will love you unconditionally. Jesus can, and

He will, deliver you – if only You open your heart to Him.

Restored to the Image of God

Nothing in life is beyond God's power and ability. You can receive God's healing and validating touch through Jesus. You were created for victory recovery, wholeness, and breakthrough! Once you open your heart to God, He will breathe life into every dead thing in your life. God will speak to the insufficiencies and hurts in your experiences, restoring your true image of Him. Just as He created man and woman in His image in the beginning of time, He will recreate you in His image in today's time.

Ladies, your Heavenly Father loves you and will always be present with you.

Now that you've read the insight given in this book, you are equipped with the proper tools to move forward into your purpose and destiny. You will no longer settle for less than what a Queen deserves.

- You Are a "Queen" and not a "Fling"

- You Are Healed and Whole

- You Are a Child of God

- You Are Not Your Past

- You Are Not a Victim, but a Victor

- You Are What God Says You Are

Now, go forth as Queens, impacting the world as God intended. And don't forget to position yourself to receive the love you deserve!

About the Author

Lestine Bell is a highly sought after dynamic keynote inspirational speaker, author, life coach to women, gifted orator and ordained minister. She is the Founder & CEO of *Lestine Bell Ministries* & *The Let's Go Inc.*, which help individuals move from being Stuck to Starting and from Pain to Purpose! She is passionately committed to empowering women to discover all of their hidden gifts and talents, so they will make a solid impact in the world. Her life changing strategies have led women all over the country to discover their hidden gifts and talents, and discovering their purpose.

Lestine has traveled the country speaking at conferences, seminars, church events, radio & television shows, helping others to maximize their full potential and to realize their God-given purpose. Known as a strong leader in the community, she was recognized in 2008 by The King Family receiving the coveted Coretta Scott King Humanitarian Award for *Outstanding Leadership*.

In 2013, she released her first book, <u>You Are Called to be a Queen & Not a Fling</u>, which helps women to embrace their worth and to overcome the pain of their past and unhealthy relationships. Lestine is devoted to help women embrace their God-given worth and value through personal and spiritual development. A woman who has overcome tremendous pain and trauma from childhood is now committed to help others overcome their challenges in life.

Let's Go, Inc. Dallas, Texas

90440959R00051

Made in the USA
Lexington, KY
11 June 2018